PUBLIC SPEAKING TOPIC SECRETS

For College, Community, Toastmasters and TED Talks

Ramakrishna Reddy

Praise for this book

"Ramakrishna Reddy has demonstrated a much wanted ability to simplify the fieldwork of public speaking. The book offers lucid and practical guidance to discover the purpose and tools to a great talk anywhere, everywhere. This little book is smart and genuinely human to help people stand up and effectively share their amazing ideas and thoughts with the rest of the world.... A practitioners toolkit to public speaking"!
— Nancy Katyal, Lead Image Coach and Soft skills Trainer
www.theperfectyou.in

"Good research and simple language. References of speeches will help the audience understand the topic more appropriately. This book is indeed a great read. Ideas that have been shared in this book seem to address the basic problem of selecting a topic. Impact of the book is so much that I already got an idea for my next speech"
— Pritam Arekar, 2013 District 41 Toastmasters
Humorous Speech Champion

"I just got a million speech writing ideas after reading this book. Earlier I thought that writing a speech was difficult but now, I feel I was wrong. With every example mentioned in this book, I realized how easy it is to come up with a speech topic. Well-done Rama! You are a true and one of the best orators."
— Noelle Nams, Author of, *'It is All Because of You'*.

"The book presents an amazing amalgamation of simplicity and efficacy of ideas in selecting speech topics. The gripping speech illustrations further help the reader in weaving the ideas into a storyline. The book is written with such spontaneity that it not only acts as a guide to Public Speaking but also ensures that the reader enjoys the journey of writing a speech."

— Manisha Rana, Corporate Executive HR, ITC

Your Free Gift

As a way of saying thanks for your purchase, I'm offering a free report that's exclusive to my subscribers and newsletter readers.

Public Speaking is not that easy. My idea is to keep it simple. If anything can be simplified, it can be learned. The eBook 'Public Speaking Made Easy' is a 25-page report that will give you very specific and 'to the point' information to overcome your fear and speak like a PRO. You can download the free ebook by going to www.PublicSpeakKing.com

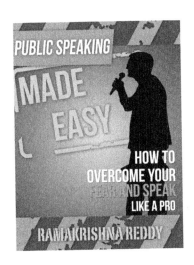

Disclaimer

No part of this publication may be reproduced or transmitted in any form or by any means, mechanical or electronic, including photocopying or recording, or by any information storage and retrieval system, or transmitted by email without permission in writing from the author/publisher.

While all attempts have been made to verify the information provided in this publication, neither the author nor the publisher assumes any responsibility for errors, omissions, or contrary interpretations of the subject matter herein.

This book is for informational purpose only. The views expressed are those of the author alone, and should not be taken as expert instruction or commands. The reader is responsible for his or her own actions.

Adherence to all applicable laws and regulations, including international, federal, state, and local governing professional licensing, business practices, advertising, and all other aspects of doing business in the US, India or any other jurisdiction is the sole responsibility of the purchaser or reader.

Dedicated to my Mom, *Ammayeammal – My guardian Angel*

ACKNOWLEDGEMENTS

I would like to thank all the toastmasters who have helped me in some way or the other. My fellow toastmasters at Infosys Pune Toastmasters Club (Pune, India), toastmasters at Aetna Speaks Up (Hartford, USA), my fellow advanced toastmasters at Central Connecticut Advanced Toastmasters (Berlin, USA). Some times we keep doing things as if we know everything. I was like that until I met *Jerry Aiyathurai*-TED Speaker and Toastmaster's World Championship Finalist. Jerry, You have been more than kind to me. I owe you a lot. I still remember you telling me to 'give' forward. I will keep up my promise. This book is one small step in keeping up with that promise. You are a Rock star! I would also like to thank the Champions, *Darren Lacroix*: 2001 World Champion of Public Speaking, *Lance Miller*: 2005 World Champion, *Dilip Abhayasekhara*: 1992 World Champion #2, from whom I have learned a ton of skills just by watching them, and interacting with them.

I want to thank my Dad *Narayana Reddy* for giving me the freedom and wisdom. I would not be the person I am today if it had not been for my three lovely sisters *Leelavathy, Lakshmi,* and *Indumathy* who took care of me after my mom aboarded to heaven. A sincere acknowledgement to my friends at school and college. You guys rock!

A big 'thank you' for the grammar queen – *Akansha Agrawal*. You are amazing and thanks for working again and again on the content. Applauds for the editor - *Charisma Srivastava*. Your quick responses and clean editing deserves a heartfelt praise. Big, big cheers to my friend, discussion panelist, cover designer, & honest critic – *Arun Prabhu*.

Finally, to you the reader: this is exciting. If it were not for you, this whole work would not hold any value.

A NOTE TO YOU, THE READER

The stage was set. Auditorium was jam-packed. I was called to the stage. I held the mike. I started to speak. "Time and tide waits for no man. So we should, so we should, hm, ah, hm, I mean', '............ thank you'. It was one of the most embarrassing moments of my life. I was in my third grade. The auditorium was full. In the same contest, my school principal's son gave a splendid talk. I remember saying to myself "Loser... Stupid"... Everybody in the school will make fun of you". I kept asking, 'If he can, why can't I'? The fact was - I had FEARs. I was really scared to face 100s of people from stage. I wanted to win this fear. But I never took any real action. Time passed by. I completed my graduation and got a job. Only after I started my career, I realized the importance of speaking and communication. Once again, I said 'hello' to my old friend - Public Speaking. I struggled for few years and then there was no looking back. This shy kid now competes at national level competitive speaking, anchors corporate events, and helps people sizzle on stage. The same kid also published multiple books selling on Amazon, creates online courses and much more. I'm no big than you or anybody. I also learnt the skills from kind people who mentored me. One of whom I can mention in every book or article is Jerry Aiyathurai. He is a fantastic mentor, amazing speaker and a genuine human being. Had it not been for him, I would not have continued to learn. I also learnt from books/courses/contests. Just that, this experience will help me to give you straightforward and simplified information. Please stick around blog / books / courses / channel of PublicSpeakKing. You'll find a wealth of information, in order to become a sizzling speaker and in turn a dynamic Leader!

For any questions, concerns, or comments, please reach out to me at Rama@publicspeakKing.com

Keep Smiling, Keep Rocking, and Happy Public Speaking.

Cheers,

Rama

TABLE OF CONTENTS

INTRODUCTION

My aim of writing this book is to give you 'specific' information so that you can get started with a solid idea for your speech. I have kept the language as conversational as possible. Over the years, I observed that the main reason people don't take up speeches is because of lack of a speech topic idea. Today, we are going to solve that problem.

I sincerely believe that this work will help anyone who wants to give a speech - Whether you are a student at school/college, or you are a social activist or you are a toastmaster. You are someone who wants to give a speech, Period. This is for you.

Often, people ask me how to select an appropriate speech topic. When questioned about why they could not find a topic, the usual reasons I hear are: *'Audience won't be interested in my speech'*, *'I am not convinced'*, *'I am not ready'*, *'I might forget the speech if I select this topic'*, *'I am not good at writing'*, etc. I believe everyone has an innate potential to speak on the platform. This work is an endeavor to spark those creative juices in your mind to find the Perfect Topic.

Do you wait for things to happen?

In general, you might want to wait for things to happen. Maybe you wait till you get that perfect speech topic idea. But from experience, I realized, waiting increases your scope to be lazy. This book is going to help you break the blocks to begin your speeches as soon as possible. You see - any good book will just provide you with good information. Unless you take action, it is not going to be of any use.

Without further ado, let's get started on finding a perfect speech topic for you.

BLUEPRINT FOR SPEECH TOPIC IDEAS

Imagine the stage is set. You are called on stage. You hear the audience applause as you walk towards the stage. The applause subsides, and you start, '*Ladies and gentlemen*'; you give an outstanding speech and say those final words '*Thank you very much*'. Your audience is rejoicing, cheering, and clapping. How does it feel? I am sure you will be thrilled. So, what is the first thing that you need to present a speech? Pat your back if you said '*A Speech Topic*'. A Speech topic is the first and foremost item that needs to be finalized for your presentation. In the past, sometimes, I thought, anything and everything could be a speech topic but most of the times, I felt all the topics were already taken! When I think **about** it now, I laugh at myself.

Let us understand the below blue print on finding a perfect speech topic.

Step 1: Larger Purpose of the speech

Some questions you can ask to find the larger purpose:
1. Why are you giving the speech?
2. What is the occasion for the speech?
3. What type of speech will suit my larger purpose?

Step 2: Topics that interest YOU

Some questions to find your interest:
1. What do you know?
2. What are you enthusiastic about?
3. What are your life experiences?

Step 3: Topics that interest Your AUDIENCE

Some questions to find your audience's interest:
1. What are your audience's needs?
2. Do they belong to a certain age group?
3. What are their shared experiences?

There are many variations of the above idea but the above has worked for me. Throughout the book, our aim is to strike that sweet spot of 'PERFECT TOPIC'

According to Toastmasters International, general or larger purpose of any speech can be classified into the following four types of speeches.

1. Informational
2. Entertaining
3. Persuasive
4. Inspirational

The aim of the first step in our blueprint will be to identify your speech's larger purpose. Before we do that, let us understand the types of speeches.

Informational Speeches: As the name suggests, these are speeches about a specific subject. You will give an informational speech when your objective is to help the audience gain knowledge on the particular subject, or strengthen their current knowledge level. Example: Project findings, 'How-to' speeches

Entertaining Speeches: People like to laugh and if you can make them laugh from the stage, you will go a long way as a speaker. You can convey a point in a straight forward way or in an entertaining way. You might have seen speeches, which are given in an entertaining fashion. Stand-up acts will fall under entertaining speech category. Humorous speeches also fall under entertaining speech category.

Persuasive Speeches: These are speeches to persuade the audience to accept your point of view. These speeches make the audience think, act or feel your point. These speeches are powerful, as you will have to deal with the psychology of the audience. If you have seen Barack Obama's acceptance or nomination speeches, they are perfect examples for persuasive speeches. Humor is also usually used in a persuasive speech. Motivational humorists use humor to entertain and persuade the audience at the same time.

Inspirational Speeches: These are speeches that will help your audience reach their highest potential. These are powerful speeches where you need to change the way your audience think/feel or act after listening to your speech. Your aim is to convince the audience to do noble things or follow greater ideologies.

Based on above information, do you get an idea of your speech's larger purpose? If not, go back to Step 1 and answer the questions. You should at least be able to tell what type of speech suits your need or requirement. Assuming your general or larger purpose is set, let us explore topic ideas that could overlap your interest and your audience's interest so that you end up with the perfect 'speech topic' idea.

Note: Even though on a higher level, speeches can be classified as Informational, Entertaining, Persuasive, and Inspiring but on a deeper level, speeches are a combination of the above. And also the speech topic ideas given in this book are not restricted to the respective type of speeches. For example, if a topic under informational speech section sparks a speech topic idea for persuasive/inspirational/humorous speech, then you should go for it.

INFORMATIONAL SPEECHES

To present an informational speech, you need to have knowledge about a subject. But it does not mean that you should have done a Post Doctorate in the subject. I am pretty sure you might be an expert in something or the other. The simple question you can ask, *'Are my audience members 'uninformed' about a particular subject?'* Then ask a question – *'How will this topic help my audience?'* The moment you ask this question, you will start thinking from your audience's perspective and you will know the appropriate information to be used in the speech.

Let us explore some speech topic ideas for informational speeches.

Things You Like:

Let us be honest. When will you give a speech? When you are excited, right? But you will only be excited, when the topic piques your interest. But the question that stops us from selecting a topic is: 'What if the audience is not interested in the topic?' I agree, not all the things that might interest you will be a suitable speech topic. So, let us explore some ideas, which are largely relatable to everyone.

Books: Assuming you are a book reader, Can you speak about why one should keep reading books? Can you write 5 major benefits of reading books? Depending upon the audience's age group, can you suggest different options? Can you talk about your favorite book? Can you inform about the importance of reading a particular book?

Gardening: If Gardening is your area of interest, can you write a speech on why gardening? Can you give tips on how to maintain a good garden? What are all the features of a good garden? What are the benefits of a good garden? Does it give you joy? What are the challenges? Every question in itself can lead to a speech of its own. Think about it.

Exercise: Can you talk about the 3 to 5 major benefits of regular exercise? How have you benefited from it? How does it help you in your day-to-day activities? What are the options available for proper exercise in the current day hectic scenario? What dieting habits to follow when you are in an exercise program? Take these questions in the direction you want. You *will* come up with an idea for your speech.

Sports: What sports do you follow or play? Based on the needs of the audience, you can frame your speech. If they are school students, you can talk about the benefits of playing a sport. If your audience members are adults, you can talk about encouraging their children to play sports. You can as well, talk about the options available for coaching; who are the different coaches, whereabouts of different training centers, or how to get enrolled in an academy.

Cooking: Are you a food aficionado? How does it help you? Please don't tell me – 'To Eat'! I am expecting something on the lines of cooking. What are some of the best practices in cooking? What are some quick ways to prepare food? What are the advantages of 'Slow Cooking'? *Do you get the idea?* The more specific the information – the more effective your speech will be.

Psychology: Does psychology fascinate you? Topics related to psychology are by and large interesting. Can you tap into the variations and specifics of the same? For example, you can explore 'Buying patterns of Consumers, 'Huge Discount on the Thanks Giving Day', 'Why Women Reject Men!' etc. *You get the idea?*

Internet: You might be an avid Internet user. This might be a very broad topic. Can you talk about any one particular aspect? Say, you want to address the privacy issue? Say you want to talk about 'Online Marketing', or you can talk about 'Preventive measure to keep away from Hackers' or how social life is changing because of advent of 'Social Media'. *Does this spark any creative juices?*

Expert: If you are an expert at what you are doing, you can inform your audience of the same. For example, if you are in the insurance industry, you can explain how your industry works in layman terms. Create the speech as if you are informing a 3rd grade student. I bet your audience will not lose you even if your information is very specific to your niche.

Observations:

We all read newspapers/magazines. At least we might browse through them. Ok, if you are not into it, at least you might watch television. Now I can hear you say 'Yes'.

Media is 'Gold' for selecting topics because it always posts topics that are current.

Go to your nearby book shop or library. Just browse through the latest magazines. Mainly check for magazines in Health/ relationships / money category. I think it is ok even if you don't buy them. We are only looking for ideas. I am pretty sure this one exercise can give you enough ideas to come up with a speech topic.

Let us take different scenarios.

You see an article that 'Using too much cell phone is not good for your health'. Maybe, even you share the same sentiment. Are you for or against it? You can take three or four main points and support them with data/facts/experiences.

You read an article that obesity has increased at alarming rates. Do you know someone who was affected by obesity? You don't necessarily need anyone in your life to be affected. You can talk about the ill effects of obesity. Or you can create a talk on how to tackle obesity. You can cite 3 or 4 major points.

There is a 'get healthy' article on Vegan diet. And say, you try it out. Can you frame a speech about your experience and inform the audience about the same? The larger idea will be to inform about the benefits of a Vegan diet with your story as the backdrop.

You watched a movie this weekend. Can you form a speech based on this movie? It need not be a review of the movie. Maybe, you took some lessons from that movie and implemented it. Will this information help the audience as well? Do you have a favorite movie/director/actor who you admire? Can you form a speech to inform why you admire him or her?

Do you watch advertisements on television? Do you have an opinion on whether the advertisements are bad/good? What do you think? Ask more people about their opinion. Keep jotting down the content. After a while, you will have enough content to give a full-blown speech.

You observe that the traffic has increased multi-fold. You find more people suffering from health issues caused by air/noise pollution. Do you want to talk about the ill effects of the same? Your speech can be to spread awareness on the same. Now, think from your perspective and come up with your angle.

If you watch NEWS channels for a week or so, I think you will have loads and loads of speech topics. Say, you see a product in the NEWS for a period of time? Have you seen a pattern? Is it in the news for good or bad? Can you collect relevant information and form a speech to inform your audience?

Do you see the Discovery channel? Does any phenomenon fascinate or interest you? Examples could be – how a vaccine protects our body, how photosynthesis helps the plants to produce food or how sunlight gets transformed into solar power. *Are your creative juices getting triggered to select more topics on this line?*

Let us observe the Geography of our habitat. Is the place where you live susceptible to heat/cold? Is there a natural calamity that is hitting time and again? Is your area or state prone to such calamities? Can you form a speech to inform on the 'What' aspect, 'Why' aspect or 'How to deal' aspect?

Problem/Solution:

Problem is one thing that we all have in common: Every single day we face problems/challenges. I am pretty sure you faced problems and found solutions as well. Would it be a good idea to share your stories on how you solved the problem? I think it would be a great idea!

You were looking for a car and you finally got a good deal. What process did you go through? How did you tackle the salesman effectively? What homework did you do before you went to the showroom? Do you think this information would help if any of your audience members wants to buy a car?

Maybe you had a wonderful vacation this year. But, before going on vacation, you were clueless. So you did a lot of research on the best deals/best places/best time of the year to visit/best mode of transport. Can you structure this information and deliver a speech?

You can talk about common health issues such as diabetes. Maybe you had it. Did you use proper dieting habits or alternative approaches? How did you overcome it? What results did you get? Can you organize the information so that your audience members can benefit?

Do you know someone who was heavy in weight but achieved a lean figure in a short period of time? Maybe it was you. What are the steps you took? What are some key things that one should follow to start building a lean figure? What should one be doing after forming a lean figure? You can take it to any level. But I bet speeches where you give a solution are always revered.

Have you felt stressed, tired and restless? You started finding ways to be energetic. Now you lead a productive and complete life. Can you call it 'Stress management'? What were your observations? Can you form a speech on citing the problem, and then giving a solution?

Have you been through a rough phase in your relationship with your loved one? Did you bounce back later? Can you share information on how you bounced back? What are all the options available out there? If someone in your audience is going through this phase, they also might be interested to know about the same. The relationship could as well be with your co-worker, your boss or your friend. Think from this aspect and I am pretty sure it might spark an idea here or there.

Did you want a website of your own? Whether you took someone's help or you learned to create one, can you form a 'How to' speech on building a website? This idea need not be about building a website. It could be 'how to rebuild your home'. It could be 'how to shoot a professional video'. Any practical information on 'How to' would be a very good idea for an informational speech topic.

Let us see an example of an Informative Speech

SPEECH SCRIPT: Sleep

It was my database management training class. *Mr. Venky* - our highly enthusiastic tutor advanced to the first row of the class and repeated the same concept again and again in a louder tone. This unusual act caught everyone's attention in the class. *Vamsi*, my friend who sat next to me was nudging me so that I opened my eyes to see our tutor standing right in front of me - shouting about a concept just to wake me up.

Ladies and Gentlemen, the reason why I told my classroom incident was not to justify why I am dumb in Database management concepts till date but to illustrate that I did not have enough sleep the previous night. All living things are subject to this phenomenon called 'Sleep'.

Have you ever wondered what causes sleep? Let me explain.

Sleep occurs based on the biological clock. We have dedicated sensors on the retina that deliver the daytime/nighttime message directly to a gland tucked deep inside the brain. In response to darkness, this tiny brain tissue produces the sleep-inducing hormone melatonin, broadcasting the message to brain areas that govern everything from body temperature to protein synthesis to hormone production to alertness.

Have you ever wondered what exactly happens when we hit the sack?

Once we close our eyes, we are subjected to two types of sleep.

The first one is NREM - Non Rapid Eye Movement sleep. This is the dreamless sleep. The NREM sleep has three major stages

Drowsiness is Stage 1. It lasts just for five or ten minutes. And in this stage our eyes move slowly under the eyelids, muscle activity slows down and we are easily awakened.

Stage 2 is Light Sleep. In this stage, our eye movements' stop, heart rate slows, and body temperature decreases.

At Stage 3, we reach Deep Sleep - It becomes difficult to awaken us at this stage, and if somebody tries to do that and succeeds, we do not adjust immediately and often feel groggy and disoriented for several minutes. I was told that I refused to move out of my room when my friend, *Albin* tried to wake me up when there were earthquake tremors in my city. Deep sleep allows the brain to go on a little vacation needed to restore the energy we expend during our waking hours.

The next type of sleep is the REM (Rapid Eye movement) sleep where our brain is as active as it was when we were awake which means our body temperature rises, the forebrain starts working trying to analyze random information thrown before it. In other words we are in dreamland. My parents used to tell me that while sleeping I used to shout something like 'Howzaaaat…. Catch it quick…. hit it'. I always thought that something was wrong with me, but recently only I realized it was all due to mechanism of REM sleep. REM is the period when we fly without wings, we spend without earning and our most fancied wishes and desires come true.

Each sleep stage is important for overall quality of sleep, but 'Deep sleep' and 'REM sleep' are especially vital. During 'Deep sleep' blood flow to the brain decreases and redirects it towards the muscles, restoring physical energy. It is this time where our immune system gets some time to be healed. Have you ever observed that whenever you are done with a big project or a series of exams you get cold or experience body pain? Well, at least now you should know this is not an accident and for all right reasons is mostly due to lack of 'Deep Sleep'. 'REM sleep' helps in cell division and protein synthesis, which aid in repairing the muscles, human growth hormone is also released during sleep. This is the reason why children should sleep for more number of hours.

The biggest sleep robber of all, however, is work—the puritan ethic has gone haywire in an era of global markets. To accommodate the relentless pressure for productivity, we're sleeping less and spending less time in social and leisure pursuits, which result in more stress and that, can steal away even more sleep.

I am not sure if it's feasible for you all to heed to my request to go to sleep on time and maintain consistent sleeping habits. But I will go home, have a hot bath, eat supple food and have a good night's sleep so that I feel energetic and fully alert to take on tomorrow's challenge.

ENTERTAINING SPEECHES

These are speeches where you want the audience to have a good time. Let us face it. If you want the audience to have a good time, you have to make them laugh. Stand-up acts, humorous speeches, feel good inspiring speeches will fall under this category.

The main ingredient that we need to master is HUMOR. Every entertaining speech will have HUMOR but the degree will vary based on whether it is a stand-up act or just a humorous speech to inform/inspire/motivate the audience.

Even though - how to create humor is out of scope of this work, I would touch base on it at a very high level.

To create entertaining speeches, you need to learn new skills. You need to learn to create a joke. You need to understand the delivery of a joke as well.

Humor is largely based on two principles:

    1. Truth

    2. Surprise.

The joke below usually gets a laugh for me. Let us understand the different parts of a joke.

<u>For people who know me, I am Rama. For people who don't know me,</u> <Pause 1> I am still Rama <Pause 2>

The underlined part is the Premise of the joke: Premise is the information needed for audience to understand your joke. Pause 1 is needed to build the tension. The following words 'I am still Rama' is the punch. The audience will laugh only after the punch line. Pause 2 is to give time for the audience to laugh.

As a rule of thumb, the premise should be true and should not be funny.

The punch should have the surprise. It can have exaggeration as well. Hearing the punch, audience will laugh.

For video illustration, please check out http://PublicSpeakKing.com/create-humor.

To learn about a simple and effective tool, please check out http://PublicSpeakKing.com/rule-of-three

Even though, many say it is difficult to come up with a topic for an entertaining speech, I think it is not 'that' difficult. Entertainment is all about making people laugh. So, if you are able to laugh at something, you can transform that as laughter matter for your audience as well. All I am trying to say is – you can create HUMOR from your own life experiences. You need not look for jokes in a joke book or from someone else's material. If something can make you laugh, why not use the same concept in your speech.

Let us explore some speech topic ideas for entertaining speeches.

Self-Deprecating:

Largely Relatable Unexpected Events:

Let us understand this with an example. Let us say, you are a guy and you are going on a date. Maybe you are a girl and you are taking a guy on a date. It is possible. Let us not rule this out! On the way, your vehicle ran out of fuel. And it turned out to be the worst date. I am pretty sure; you will share this incident with your buddies at the coffee table. Just note the way you describe the incidents to your friends. Note down the instances and sentences at which they laugh. Jot down the exact sentences. It will be easier to create an entertaining speech.

Unusual Physical Traits:

Your physical traits are what the audience will see at the first place. If someone else uses your physical trait, then it becomes offensive. If you self-depreciate your own physical trait, it is comedy! Just think what is unique about your appearance. Are you very tall, good looking, not so good looking? Write down instances where you had embarrassing experiences / funny experiences because of that trait. Let us see an example.

I have seen a speech, where the speaker won the Humorous Speech Championship at toastmasters just with one idea. 'He was short'. He constructed the whole plot with his height. He shared his embarrassments since he was a child. He cited funny incidents at school and public places. He described his relationship with his wife who was taller than him. It was a laughter riot. What ideas does this give you?

Are you dark in color? I don't want you to spark any racist feelings. Only if others talk about your color, it can be called as racism. If 'you' joke about your color, it is not racism. There must be certain instances where you were embarrassed or had unique experiences because of your color. This could be your idea for entertaining speech topic.

Your Current Life Situation:

Think about your current life situation. In whatever stage of life you are currently in, you could easily form topics. For example,

Are you a teenager? You can talk about your experience with your 'girl' friends. It does not mean, you need to have one. Even if you don't have one, write how hard it is to have one. If you have a girl friend, write how hard it is to maintain one!

Are you in your 20s? Can you talk about your quarter life crisis? Maybe you are not happy with your job. Maybe you don't want to get married. Maybe you want to get married but are scared. May your got married! In that case, I think your every day life will be material for your entertaining speech! Just complain!

Even if you are in 30s, 40s, or 50s, I am sure some part of your current life situation worries you. By being real and authentic, you build trust and credibility with the audience. This is very important to create humor. And humor is the main ingredient in an entertaining speech.

16

Your Identity:

By far, the best entertaining speeches are the ones when the speaker builds instant credibility with the audience. One way to build credibility is to pick topics related to your country, religion, or culture. If 'you' do it, it is ok. Only if anyone else does it, it becomes a controversy.

Are you from a particular country or ethnic group? For example, Chinese are famous for low cost manufacturing. Indians are famous for software industry. United States is famous for outsourcing. What is your country famous for? What are the characteristics of people in your country or group that amuses you? If you find it funny, chances are the audience also may find it funny.

Are you from a particular religion? Even though religion is a taboo topic, I think it is ok to talk about the truth of one's own religion. There are always misconceptions/false beliefs in the name of religion. Have you felt that before? Can you jot down instances of the same? The legendary George Carlin's stand up on Religion is a masterpiece. It might spark an idea or two for you.

Are you from a group/race that speaks or pronounces English language in a different way? For example, Chinese speak English with a lot of accent. Africans have a different accent. Europeans have a different accent. I think Russell Peters is an expert in this area. You should watch his stand-ups to get some practical ideas.

Characters in your life:

Characters in your family:

From observation and experience, entertaining speeches related to your family usually click. I would recommend you to watch Kevin Hart's 'Laugh At My Pain' (Check YouTube). Most of his acts are related to his dad, son, and daughter. You can learn tons and tons about comedy by watching his one show.

Let us relate to different scenarios.

Do you have *interesting* conversations with your Dad? His point of view and your point of view are totally different? Or your Mom is super religious. And you are not. The contradiction plays a major role in entertainment.

Do your Grand Parents ask ridiculous questions that you cannot answer? Do you feel there is a generation gap? Do you get frustrated?

Do you have younger brother/sister who drives you crazy all the time?

The responsibility of raising a baby might scare someone. Do you have a small child who irritates you?

Just to give an example, See 'Louis C.K Why?' in YouTube (http://bit. ly/stsent)

Are you a Dad or a Mom? Do babies scare you? This might sound weird but it is true.

Do you have teenage children who don't listen to you? You have a topic for an entertaining speech.

The mother of all topics: Your better half. Maybe it is your Boyfriend/ Girlfriend. Or it could be your husband/wife. Let us assume; you have a Girl Friend or a wife. By and large, even though this topic is widely pervasive in entertainment world, it still works. You need a proof? Look at the number of romantic comedies in Hollywood, Oh my God! So, my point is you can select this as your topic.

Maybe the instances with the characters happened in the past. It is ok. If someone can laugh listening to your story, chances are that your audience might as well laugh at your speech.

Characters in your professional life:

Is there a boss or a co-worker who is weird? Frame a speech around how that character annoys you or how that character amuses you. I am pretty sure similar characters are in your audiences' lives as well.

Did you face any strict professor or teacher who gave you a hard time?

How was your experience with him or her?

Characters in social setting:

You have a friend whose actions entertain you all the time. Can you decode the instances and nuances on what are his or her characteristics? Can you form a speech out of the same?

Did a car salesman rip you off? Or for that matter, did any salesman rip you off? I am pretty sure, your audience would also relate to the same. Can you create HUMOR based on your experience with the salesman?

Did you ever have a tiff with a cab driver/auto driver? Does this sound like material for your speech?

Did you meet an unruly waiter at a food joint? Did he scare you before even you ordered the food? Try to think of your experience with Flight attendants, Tele marketers, Shop keepers, etc.

Alert: You should understand that we are only discussing speech topic ideas. Writing and delivering humor is a totally different ball game.

SPEECH SCRIPT: Story of a Software Engineer

For people who know me, I am Rama. For people who don't know me, I am still Rama.

I am a software professional. But software was not my ambition. As a child, I wanted to be a rock star. There is a wide spread exaggeration that parents in India pressure you to only become a doctor or an engineer. That's not true. They don't pressure. They blackmail. If you tell your dad, 'I want to be a rock star', you will be smacked left and right and hear things like, how will you get married? They talk as if the ultimate aim of you growing up is to get married, which is not bad, if you get a rich, beautiful and obedient girl.

As a teenager, I wanted a lot of money for outing, partying and flirting.

You see, my dad did not give me any money but he gave me a lot of value. My dad is an honest, self-made and respected man. My dad is a hard nut to crack.

I would say, 'Dad, Can you buy me a motorcycle?'

No

Can I go for an overnight party?

No

Can you at least buy me a cell phone?

No

No. I didn't even say anything.

You see, my dad did not give me necessary things like money but he gave me a lot of unnecessary things like advice. He said, 'Study well, get a good job, you can buy anything you want'. I studied well. I got a good job. I wanted to buy my favorite motorcycle – Kawasaki Ninja. I went to the showroom. I checked the prices. It was depressing. Don't you think that the things you really, really want always cost you more money: Think about it. That beautiful house, that beautiful car, that beautiful girl always cost you more money. Back at the showroom, a sales guy figured out I was a software guy. He said, 'Sir, this bike is perfect for you'. I said, 'I know. But I don't have enough money'. He goes, 'No problem sir. We will apply a loan against your salary'. I said, 'No'. Don't you think it is weird that sometimes we start telling our financial situation even though it is not needed? I am telling him, 'I don't get the salary which you think I get'. I think that the sales guy started feeling good about his job.

You see - Money is not the problem. Lack of more money is always the problem.

So to get more money, I went to my dad. On a Friday evening, my dad and I were having a good time. We were having tea.

'Dad, I am buying a bike. Can you give me some money?'

Guess what he said, 'No' but I can give you a solution.

I said, 'What?'

He goes, 'Get married'.

I said, 'Why?'

'You will get a bike and also a girl'.

But you know what was stupid about me? I said, 'No'. I wanted to earn my own money. So, now – I went to my boss. I said, 'Boss, I need more money'. He goes, 'Ha Ha Ha'. He said 'I will apply your US VISA.' I got excited. But my VISA got rejected. Not once but twice. I got dejected. Trust me; it was more painful than being rejected by a girl. Nothing was happening in my life. So, I went to an NGO for suicide prevention, as a volunteer. Now, my problems seemed much smaller. If you are like me, 'Listen close. Stop Running. Things will happen'. Guess what happened next, the third year: my VISA got approved. I went to United States: I didn't buy a bike but I bought my favorite car.

I invited my dad to United States. As a proud son, I picked him up in my car. He looked into my eyes and said, 'Rama, When will you get married'?

PERSUASIVE SPEECHES

For persuasive speeches, you need to convince the audience to take some action or change their perception based on your point. I think most of the people today need someone else to confirm what is the right thing to do. And when you tap into this fact, you will easily find speech topics for persuasion. Before we explore topic ideas for persuasive speeches, it is a good idea to know about ethos, pathos and logos. The great philosopher Aristotle coined these terms. These terms are different elements involved in persuasion. In a nutshell:

1. *Ethos* relates to the credibility quotient- being fair, using proper language, using correct grammar, using appropriate vocabulary.

2. *Pathos* relates to the emotional quotient - emotional tone, stories of emotional events

3. *Logos* relate to the logical quotient - facts or figures, citing history, logical arguments.

Ideally, every persuasive/inspiring speech should have these three elements. Personally, I believe that ethos and pathos play a very important role in a persuasive/inspiring speech. By far the best way to incorporate ethos and pathos is to tell a personal *Story*. Mark Brown, 1995 World Champion of Public Speaking conducted by TI* said, 'Your life tells a story and there is someone out there who needs to hear it'. As a rule of thumb, if pathos is not high, you can use ethos to the major extent instead of logos. But highly skilled speakers can also use logos to the major extent to persuade the audience.

Let us explore some speech topic ideas for persuasive speeches.

My mentor *Jerry Aiyathurai* (2005 Finalist in International Speech contest) asked me to answer the below questions:

Who are you? What do you think this life is all about? What is your message about it?

His words struck a chord with me. If you answer these questions with stories, you will have enough speech topic ideas for Persuasive speaking.

What are your core values? List them down. *Who taught them to you? When did that happen? What are the things you used to believe in?* List them down. Did any particular incident change those beliefs? When did that happen? How did that change, change your life?

What were your most painful periods in your life? How did you overcome them? What did you learn from them? *What is your message?*

World Champion of Public Speaking (WCPS) Reference Ideas:

WCPS 1986: *Arabella Bengson's* speech 'We can be Pygmalion' was to persuade the audience to 'encourage' people. Pygmalion was a Greek sculptor who gave life to his statue. She used Pygmalion as a metaphor to convey this point. She used her son's story and also cited relevant examples of Helen Keller and her mentor. Was this a really hard message that only Arabella could have shared? No – You or I can also write a persuasive speech on how to encourage others. She felt that 'encourage others' was her core message. *What actions do you value in your life?* List down stories that stirred your emotion.

WCPS 1988: *Jerry Starke's* 'Please don't walk on Mother's Roses' was to persuade young adults not to tell the problems of the heart to their parents. He shared his own story of how he and his wife became empty nesters and then their children again started coming up to them to share their problems. Is this a very unique story? Not really but Jerry could create a Championship speech based on this idea. *What do you want to convey to your audience? What did your life teach you?*

WCPS 2005: *Lance Miller's* speech 'The Ultimate Question' (http://bit.ly/stslance) was to persuade the audience to validate the goodness in others. His speech was about an incident involving a parking ticket that changed his life. He persuades us to follow the same and change our life for the better. In a workshop, Lance joked that he used to feel; something tragic should happen to him so that he could write a powerful persuasive speech. *What incident (even simple) changed your life?* Write what was your core learning, and write a speech on how it changed your life.

WCPS 2006: *Ed Hearn's* speech 'Bouncing back' was to persuade people to devise a strategy to bounce back when life throws challenges at you. He used his childhood story about his punching bag. This punching bag was the protagonist in his speech, which symbolized the concept of bouncing back. This speech gives us an idea where things and objects that are close to our lives can also be source of our speech topics. *What are the things/objects that are dear to you? What does it really mean to you? What difference did it make in your life?*

TED/TEDˣ Speech Reference Ideas:

Simon Sinek's speech, 'How leaders Inspire action' (http://bit.ly/ stssimsinek) on leadership was to persuade the audience that great leaders Martin Luther King, Steve Jobs, Wright brothers always started with 'Why?' He wants the audience to build or make decisions based on 'Why'. A concept of this simplicity made Simon an in demand speaker. *What is your philosophy that you want to tell your audience?*

Dan Pink's 'The puzzle of motivation' (http://bit.ly/stsdanpink) was to persuade the audience that traditional rewards are not as effective as what the managers think. He uses apt stories to illustrate his point and persuade the audience to think differently. *Do you have a point, which is against the status quo?* Find stories to illustrate that point. It can be yours or from external sources.

Eli Pariser's speech 'Online filter bubbles' (http://bit.ly/stselipar) persuades the audiences to beware of the web companies that tailor their services to our personal tastes. His argument was to persuade the audience that this phenomenon has deprived them of seeing a broader picture. This is a relevant topic for the current times. *What are the trends that you find to be disturbing the population at large?* Have you seen any phenomenon that is or will be causing a major problem? What is your argument? How do you want the audience to think/act or feel differently?

Stefan Larson's speech 'What doctors can learn from each other' (http://bit.ly/stsstelar) persuades the doctor/hospital communities at large to share data with each other in order to bring on a healthcare revolution where healthcare could be better and cheaper. What industry do you work in? Are you a teacher or lawyer or just a student? *Do you have any specific ideas that you want to implement?* Can you form the thesis on that point and persuade the audience?

Jeff Speck's speech 'The walkable city' (http://bit.ly/stsjefspec) was about solving the problem of suburbs. His speech was to persuade the audience to accept his idea of designing a walkable city.

Well, you might not be an urban planner or someone of that caliber but *do you have an idea for a day-to-day problem?* This idea could be the one to build a persuasive speech.

Jonas Eliasson's speech 'How to solve traffic jams' (http://bit.ly/stsJoneli) is about solving the problem of the peak hour congestion. He shares the successful experiments done in his home city 'Stockholm' to solve the traffic congestion and shares the results. He persuades the audience that we just need to nudge people to accept ideas instead of telling them to adapt to new ideas. *What experiments have you done in your life?* Do you get any ideas for a persuasive speech?

Arthur Benjamin's speech 'Teach statistics before calculus' (http://bit.ly/W1amSX) is against the status quo of the education system. He persuades the audience that statistics should be taught before calculus so that it is relevant in the digital age. This is a very simple idea but imagine the impact it could make if it is implemented. His point is right. We don't use calculus in real life as much as we use statistics. Does this trigger any idea in your mind? How many courses have you studied? Do you use every topic in real life? What subjects used in real life should be taught at school? Can you form a speech based on your argument?

Esther Duflo's speech 'Social Experiments to fight poverty' (http://bit. ly/stsestduf) is an informative and persuasive speech on the distribution of Aid to fight poverty. She gave a solution of 'Randomized testing trials' and answers some specific questions that prove that the aid was distributed successfully. Her persuasion is to follow the 'Randomized testing trials' to fight against poverty and distribution of financial aid. She persuades the audience that there is a solution that you can discover if you experiment at lower level where risks are minimal. *Do you have any solution and you are skeptical whether your solution would work or not?* Why not try experimenting and form a speech out of it?

William Li's speech 'Can we eat to starve cancer?' (http://bit.ly/stswilli) was to persuade the audience to think about treating cancer and other diseases by eating the cancer-fighting foods so that it prevents the growth of blood vessels that feed the cancer tumor. Even though this is a simple solution – this can change the way the audience thinks about fighting cancer. *Did you ever get an idea that you felt could act as a solution to any serious problem?* What is that idea? Can you persuade the audience to accept your idea to solve the problem?

Juan Enriquez's speech 'Your online life, permanent as a tattoo' (http://bit.ly/stsjuaenr) was about the changes in the digital space. He persuades the audience to have a better perception of their online identity. His argument is that online identify remains forever even after you're gone – kind off making you immortal. He weaves the whole speech with stories from Greek legends. Even though the speech is short, he uses metaphors and anecdotes in the best possible way to persuade the audience. *What is your perception of the current trends in the world?* This speech is one of best use of 'logos' element of persuasion.

Graham Hill's speech 'Less stuff, more happiness' (http://bit.ly/ stsgrahil) is a beautiful concept where he persuades the audience to have less stuff and less space to create more and more happiness. He also goes ahead and gives three rules that the audience can use to edit one's life. These are the topics that excite me. They are so simple, so relatable and so practical. At a fundamental level, even you or I know that we don't need a lot of stuff to be happy. Is this topic triggering any idea for you to build upon a persuasive speech? How about 'Sell your mansion and live in a caravan'. I was kidding. I am sure you got the idea.

Matt Cutts's speech 'Try something new for 30 days', (http://bit. ly/stsmatcut) as the title says was to persuade the audience to try something new for 30 days. He persuaded the audience by sharing his own example. He followed this advice, which was given by American philosopher Morgan Spurlock. Even though he is an engineer at Google, he had authored a book. He climbed Mt. Kilimanjaro. He also did not have sugar for 30 days. He uses the logic – If I can do it, you can do it. Does this logic apply to anything in your life? *What results have you produced by sticking to any habit?* Can you persuade the audience with the same argument? This will prove to be a good use of 'ethos' and 'logos' to persuade your audience.

Nilofer Merchant's speech 'Got a Meeting. Take a walk' (http://bit. ly/stsnilmer) is one of the sweetest and simplest persuasive speeches I have come across. She persuades the audience to have your one-to-one meeting as a walking meeting! If you think about it, this is a great message. Her point: 'Walking' triggers out of the box ideas and also helps you get better health. Does this trigger any idea?

What simple things do you suggest to people? Are you a propagator of 'No Smoking', 'No Sugar', or 'No Junk food'? Simple messages go a long way to create an impact and persuade the audience.

Munir Virani's speech 'Why I love vultures' (http://bit.ly/stsmunvir) is to persuade the audience that vultures are one of the critical species, which maintain the balance in our eco-system. Since vultures are perceived in a negative context in our day-to-day lingo, he persuades the audience to change their perception about vultures. This is a persuasive speech where the speaker wants to shift the thought process of the listeners so that they take this idea forward. *Do you have a point that goes against a common perception?*

SPEECH SCRIPT: Only Three Doors

This January, my manager put me in charge of a critical project. Being a fairly ambitious guy, I worked day-in and day-out to get that most awaited promotion. I was exhausted.

A few weeks ago, at five in the morning, the phone jangled me awake. As soon as I picked up the call, I heard 'Why didn't you call me?' Don't you remember I exist? Do you love me? These questions were fired for the third time in the past three months by my third girlfriend. I am just kidding; by my one and only girlfriend, *Lavanya*

Ladies and gentlemen, relationships are hard and the ones with people we truly love can be particularly hard. But at that point, all I wanted was some sleep! Exhausted, I fell back asleep but not completely. I was half awake and half asleep. In that state, I felt some part of me was out of my body. Have you been there? I was in such a situation for the third time in the past three months. Some part of me cried for help. And every time it did, I saw three doors with a note on them that read, 'Listen when you open the door'.

The first time I chose door one. Why? Well, I had to choose some door. Inside door one; I saw a movie being screened. I saw glimpses of my life situation where things went my way. Everybody listened to me! My ego loved it. I got excited instantly, feeling how great I am and how fortunate *Lavanya* was to have me as her boyfriend.

I called *Lavanya* and said, 'Don't you know how hard I am working? Don't you know how important my role is?'

Lavanya said, 'Yes, I know how important you are, Idiot'

What?

I didn't expect that. We had what we call a high volume discussion. My relationship was not working.

The second time I chose door two because door one was not working! Inside door two, I saw another movie being screened. Guess who was in the movie? It was me again. I saw my life situations where I apologized to run away from the situation. I picked up my phone and said '*Lavanya*, I am sorry. Please don't make this an issue' I was sure that *Lavanya* would feel better.

Lavanya said, 'I, I am making an issue'. "What do you think *Rama*? You say sorry and I will forgive you? Now, I really felt like an, Idiot. We had a low volume discussion. This was worse. My relationship was still not working.

The third time, I didn't want *Rama*'s ego in door one. I didn't want *Rama*'s Apology in door two. I wanted a better outcome. I entered door three. Inside door three, No movie was being screened. Now, I chose to listen. When I called *Lavanya*, I listened to her anger, I listened to her hurt, but then I heard something beautiful, for what we could be.

'You are missing me right? It feels so great to hear your voice honey'. I sensed solemn silence. I melted, and so did *Lavanya*. And I heard something beautiful. She said,

'Yes, I missed you badly Stupid'. Through the narrow telephone line, we had found a connection.

Friends, what am I really saying here? Our connections with our loved ones are not about ego or apology but about listening. Relationships will blossom because Love Listens. I'd like to leave you with a question, the most precious people in your life might be asking of you. The question is not, how much do you love them? The question is -are you listening?

INSPIRING SPEECHES

If someone asks me what gift would I like to have as a speaker? I would say, 'The gift of 'inspiring' my audience'.

Do you realize that by your mere speech - you are influencing someone's life? Think about it. It is powerful stuff.

I still get excited about writing and delivering inspiring speeches. This is one of most profound things you can do to yourself. You know what will happen if you do that? I can guarantee that at least one person will be inspired after your speech. And that person will be YOU. You will be automatically following your message because you have created it. I cannot explain this in words but you have to feel the thrill and excitement when you create an inspiring speech. However, don't give speeches that do not resonate with you.

You have already explored topics in the earlier sections, but instead of persuading your audience to agree to your viewpoint; your core focus is to inspire them to new possibilities.

Think - when do you get inspired? That is a very important question to ask. Don't you get inspired when you 'feel' a speech? Why is it going to be different for your audience? And when would they 'feel' your speech? I think 'pathos' plays a vital role in an inspiring speech. And I believe that personal stories are very effective to use 'ethos' and 'pathos' for an inspiring speech. Don't think that you don't have content because you didn't climb Mt. Everest, or fight in a world war, or save a dying person. Someone said - if you reached adulthood, you would have more stories than you ever thought.

Once, my mentor *Jerry Aiyathurai* gave me an advice. He asked me, *to write down three surprises of my life.* When I did, BING – I got an idea that led to another and I formed an inspiring speech for a speech contest. It took a lot of iterations before I could arrive at the core thesis.

What about you? *Can you write down the three surprises of your life?* What did you learn from it?

WCPS (World Champion of Public Speaking) Speech Reference Ideas:

WCPS 1987: *Harold Patterson's* speech 'The Pain Passes' was based on the quote 'The pain passes, but the beauty remains'. He inspired the audience to embrace this message by citing the story of Wilma Rudolph and citing his own personal story. *What is your favorite quote? Do you have a story to tell to prove that quote?* Now - that is going to inspire the audience to embrace the quote so that they do better things in life.

WCPS 1989: *Dan Johnson's* speech was all about LOVE. He inspired the audience to share it and say it. He used his own family get-together as the backdrop for his speech and used humor very effectively to convey his point. *Love is an evergreen topic to inspire others.* I think that this will never become a FAD. If it had been, then Hollywood would have gone bankrupt.

WCPS 1990: *David Brook's* speech was about having Honor, Integrity and Self-respect. He inspired the audience by telling the story of the Lone Ranger. Well, it was a metaphor to put across his core message. Lone Ranger is a symbol that a Texan is very proud off. *What symbols inspire you?* How does it connect with your larger than life concepts such as Honor, Integrity or Self-Respect? Can you write down stories related to those concepts?

WCPS 1991: *Dave Ross's* speech was about Success and how to achieve it. He used examples of Abraham Lincoln, Wilma Rudolph, and Winston Churchill to inspire people to go against odds to achieve success. He inspired the audience that courage is the most important thing to achieve success. *What do you believe to be the most important thing? Who inspires you?* Can you use that as material to inspire people?

WCPS 1992: *Dana Lamon* talks about 'Taking a Chance'. He is blind.

I think this speech was a perfect mix of ethos, pathos and logos. He used logic of coming to Vegas and taking a chance at the casino to taking a chance in life. His persuasion came across as very powerful when he talked about how he took a chance during his child's birth. *What different did you do with your life, which was against the norm?* What is your message to the audience?

WCPS 1993: *Otis William Jr.'s* speech was about 'It's Possible'. He inspires the audience to achieve anything in life by following a formula DAP – Desire, Action and Perseverance. His examples for each part of the formula were very strong and clear. He had effective use of 'logos'. But the turning point in his speech was the use of 'pathos'. The story was about how he successfully defied the odds to get his promotion. *Did you follow any formula to achieve success?* Can you inspire people to use the same so that they can achieve success?

WCPS 1996: *David Nottage's* speech was 'Get Up'. The speech was to inspire the audience to get up if they were lying down after facing failure. He used two stories from his life. One from his childhood on learning to ride a bike and the other story was the difficulty he faced in his business. *What lesson was learnt earlier in your life?* How did you implement it again to overcome the situation in you life? Example 'Be honest' was something you learnt earlier in your life. What stories did you have to say about being honest? Can you inspire your audience with that message?

WCPS 2000: *Ed Tate's* speech 'One of Those Days' was very different from all the previous championship speeches. His speech was a simple story about his experience at the airport. Just by telling that simple story, he inspired the audience to 'Do the Right Thing'. *Do you have an experience that inspired you to do something great?* It could be simple things such as – Raising a voice against someone barging in a queue or Being assertive to say 'No'. Just put on your thinking hat. I am pretty sure you will get enough ideas to inspire others.

WCPS 2001: *Darren Lacroix's* speech 'Ouch' (http://bit.ly/stsdarlac)

was to persuade the audience to be willing to fail. He proposes that anything worthwhile cannot be achieved if you are not willing to fail. He used two stories. One his personal story of becoming a comedian and the other was that of a Rocket scientist, the brain behind the rocket launch to moon. I have heard Darren share how he came up with this speech. So I am sharing that idea directly so that you can use it to create your inspiring speech. It seems his mentor, 1995 World Champion Mark Brown asked Darren, 'What will be your message to your child if you were to die tomorrow'? This is powerful stuff. What message will you come up with? If you don't have children – it's ok. *What will be your message to your most loved one if you were to die tomorrow?*

WCPS 2003: *Jim Key's* speech 'Never too late' (http://bit.ly/stsjimkey) was to inspire the audience that it is never too late to follow your dreams. He used the movie 'Rookie' as the backdrop to kick off the speech. He used another story of a girl who was hearing impaired, visually impaired and a stroke survivor. He effectively used these stories to inspire the audience that it is never too late to follow your dreams. I think this is a great example where Jim chose not to be the protagonist. Instead he inspires the audience by citing the instances when he got inspired. In your life, *what inspired you and when did that happen*? Why can't that be your next inspiring speech?

WCPS 2004: *Randy Harvey's* speech 'Lessons from Fat Dad' (http://bit.ly/stsranhar) was to inspire the audience to Love. He used the story of his own childhood. He mentions how his dad nurtured him. Even though he talked about the valuable advice his dad gave to him, his main point for the audience was to 'Love'. This was a classic speech consisting of his experiences with his dad. I bet you have a family member who loves you as much as you love him or her. What has the love proved to be? *How did it change your life?* How can it change the audience's life? Can you inspire the audience for the better?

WCPS 2007: *Vikas Jhingran's* speech 'The Swami's question' (http://bit.ly/stsvikjhi) was to inspire people to find out 'who are we' to succeed in life. His thesis was that all the answers that we need to

33

succeed lie within us and not somewhere else. He used his own story to prove this point. This speech gives a philosophical message yet it is very relatable. *What philosophy do you believe in?* Write down your story to inspire people in your philosophy.

WCPS 2009: *Mark Hunter's* speech was to inspire the audience to change their inner world. He told the story about how an accident changed his life for worse. His speech was about his revelation in his life. He talks about how his perception changed after years and years of struggle. He inspires the audience by telling them about the lesson he learnt at his grandma's kitchen table. Have you gone through pain after an accident? Did you form perceptions? *Did any event happen that inspired you to change?* Can you inspire your audience to change perceptions by telling your story?

TED/TED^x Speech Reference Ideas:

Hannah Brencher's speech 'Love letters to strangers' (http://bit.ly/stshanbre) was to inspire people to spread love. She told her story where she came out of depression by sending love letters to random people in and around New York. I think this speech had the right mixture of ethos, pathos and logos. If you see, this speech was an outcome of who Hannah became. Do you resonate with this theme 'spreading love'? *What did you turn out be in life? What changed you?* Do you have stories to share that in turn can inspire the audience for the better?

Nigel Marsh's speech 'how to make work-life balance work' (http://bit.ly/stsnigmar) tears upon the extremely wide pandemic – struggling work life balance. This talk inspires people to construct their life and not let their careers construct their life. He also goes all the way to give an example of how he constructs his day. He has four major points for the audience to ponder upon. *Do you have a career? What are the things you want to change?* Have you done something about it? Does this spark an idea or two?

Sir Ken Robinson's speech 'Bring on the learning revolution' (http://

bit.ly/stskenrob) is a wonderfully crafted speech that is entertaining as well as inspiring. Ken talks about education. He believes that the current educational system is fundamentally flawed and it strips a child's creativity. He inspires the audience to believe that the current educational system needs to be revolutionized to empower the future generations. This is a powerful talk on a very important subject. *Do you strongly believe about fundamental issues?* Not necessary only someone like Ken can talk about it. If you have a story to share, you can do it too!

I am going to mention another example related to education. *Rita F Pierson's* speech 'Every kid needs a champion' (http://bit.ly/ stsritpia) fundamentally talks about the beauty of teacher and student relationships. She inspires the audience that learning takes place because of relationships. Her point is that teachers need to build relationships to inspire the students to learn. Even though the larger theme was education, her speech was not dealing with only education but it was also about relationships, about teachers, and their students. What idea does this give? Can you see how different dimensions can kick in to create an inspirational speech? Rita was an educator for 40 years so she had the credibility to speak on that topic. Maybe you have spent enough time in another area. *What dimension of your area of expertise, do you think is unheard off?* Can you give voice to that dimension?

Becci Manson's speech '(Re) touching lives through photos' (http:// bit.ly/stsbecman) was about how she touched the lives of tsunami-hit Japan by retouching the photos they had lost during the tsunami. It is a simple story of her social service for 3 weeks in Japan. This speech inspires people to go beyond their comfort zone to help people. Do you have such a story? It may not be as powerful as helping tsunami-hit survivors. It could be teaching algebra to an under privileged kid in your neighborhood. Say if you are a student, it could be the story of how you helped your fellow student? *What stories do you have to inspire people to help those in need?*

Lisa Bu's speech 'How books can open your mind' (http://bit.ly/stslisbu) inspires people to read books. Even though this can be a good topic for informational speech; Lisa used books as an inspiring speech topic. How? Lisa showed how she got in touch with herself by reading books. She proves how books helped her overcome her shattered dream. This is a beautiful speech where you learn how simple topics can be used to construct an inspiring speech. I am pretty sure some activity of yours could have solved a fundamental issue in your life. Maybe it is photography, filmmaking, acting, playing football, etc. You get the idea? List down the activity and also list down the core problem it solved in your life. Write down story on how that activity changed your life.

Amy Cuddy's speech 'Your body language shapes who you are' (http://bit.ly/stsamycud) inspires people to just fake their body language till they become what they want. The best part of the speech is that she uses humor, statistics, and stories to inspire the audience. She has a message for the world that could change the lives for better. She is a professor and her area of expertise is non-verbal communication related to power and dominance. This gives us an idea to uncover inspiring messages from what we do for a living.

Laura Trice's speech 'Remember to say thank you' (http://bit.ly/stslautri) is about how she changed from 'not saying thanks' to 'saying thanks'. She gets deep into why we don't use words of admiration and praise. She then inspires people to go ahead and use words of praise and admiration at their homes to build a better and peaceful world. This is a classic speech topic. Does this give you a new dimension to the theme of being thankful, having gratitude, or praising someone; or ideas for making someone's day better? Any of the themes could be your speech topic.

Now let us see the script for an inspiring speech.

SPEECH SCRIPT: Pursue Your Passion

On Oct. 1ˢᵗ 1993, in a packed auditorium, I walked on to the stage wearing a blue half-trouser and white half sleeve shirt. I held the mike and started a speech "Time is a gift given by God and one has to use it wise, hum, huh".

Ladies and gentlemen – that was my first public speaking experience. I bombed it and it was painful. I got determined to learn this art. So I volunteered for every stage appearance. I started to get comfortable with speaking on the stage. Even though I developed a deep liking for public speaking, I ignored it as I grew up. It was like I had a rare and precious plant in my garden. I felt good about it whenever I saw that plant but I never nurtured the plant

I completed my engineering and joined Infosys as a software engineer. Even after I joined Infosys, I only pursued my assigned work and never pursued what I really loved to do. Whenever I would see someone anchor on a stage, the child in me would wonder, '*Rama* - why are you not anchoring?' But the big boy in me said, "There are greater things to pursue in life. Better focus on that buddy". I pursued my so-called greater things in life and did not listen to that innocent child asking me to pursue my passion.

In July 2008, my US VISA got rejected. Almost everyone's VISA in my friends' circle got approved. Although nobody was to be blamed, I was sad. There was a point when I would just stare at the computer monitor and only after an hour or so would I realize that I had not completed anything. I realized that I was enduring rather than enjoying my life

In Dec 2008, I came across Toastmasters. I was fascinated by the whole idea and the enthusiasm shown by the members. At that point I realized I had never really boarded the train of my life. I let the train pass me by as if I was doing a favor to life. I wanted to change it. I joined toastmasters. I was so delighted to see the amount of enthusiasm and inspiration I got while I worked for my speeches. My blood found new joy in circulation, alertness levels touched new heights and each cell of my body displayed happiness. To be honest, I never really worked for winning but worked to deliver a speech, which was beneficial and most enjoyable to my audience. What I never expected were the awards that I won at the various contests. I reached the District level humorous speech – the highest level of competition - on my first attempt. When my manager *Rohini* heard about this, she brought it to the notice of my Senior Project Manager. After 15 minutes, I was called to my Delivery Manager *Anand's* cabin. *Anand* said "We have our Account town hall the day after tomorrow and IT heads of our client are visiting our unit. Can you host the event" After a pause, he asked," I have never seen you speak in public, would you be able to host this crucial event?" Before my mind could analyze the situation I said, "Yes, I will do it". Everything seemed to have a connection. Out of no-where, here I stood with an offer from my Delivery manager to fulfill my desire. And maybe that was the reason the response came like a blitzkrieg. All things fell in place and there I stood behind the podium and greeted our client IT heads and unit heads. The event was a success and I received warm appreciations from my senior management. It seemed like magic. I fulfilled my desire without even having a plan. I believe the universe has only one purpose, to plant the right desires and help us fulfill them. It can help, but only if we pursue it with passion. The magic is pursuing your passion.

Passion is the only elixir that we alone can produce to take care of ourselves. Whether we are an ordinary person or a celebrity, it is passion alone that determines the extent to which we are alive. I believe what *Sir Ken Robinson* said, "If you do something that resonates with your spirit, hours would seem likes minutes, if you do something that does not resonate with your spirit, minutes would seem like hours". I am not telling you to quit your job tomorrow and do things you love. My point is give time to things you love. Maybe one day you will make a living out of it. There are many things in life that would catch your eye but only some will catch your heart, and only a few would excite your spirit and energy. Pursue your passion.

CONCLUSION

You have read the book. Congratulations!

I hope you got an idea for your speech. If you are still waiting for the right time to start the speech, I have NEWS for you. Listen Close. You listening? Just get up and start writing your speech. To start off, you might not write the perfect speech. It is ok. But as Nike's tagline says 'JUST DO IT'. Speech writing and delivery is a continuous process. Neither you nor I can claim that we have mastered this skill. I believe you should start speaking whenever you get a chance. Some options are to join a toastmasters club or call rotary clubs for a speaking slot (they have speaking slots but you have to book in advance), or be a master of ceremony at functions/weddings/corporate functions/town hall/gathering.

I would be thrilled if even one idea present in this book has helped you find a speech topic. If you are thrilled as well, can you share your joy by writing an honest customer review? By doing this, you are helping someone like you who is also looking for a Speech Topic Idea. This will also help me in a great way. You can leave a review at amazon.com

Cheers,

Rama

Rama@publicspeakKing.com

CPSIA information can be obtained
at www.ICGtesting.com
Printed in the USA
LVOW04s2213061215

465696LV00024B/647/P